AUTISM IS AN EXTRAORDINARY CONDITION

Do not misjudge Autism. Learn and understand.

AUTHOR: Elena Quevedo, MD
CO-AUTHOR: Stephanie St. Marie

To order additional copies of this book, please contact:
Palibrio
1663 Liberty Drive
Suite 200
Bloomington, IN 47403
Toll Free from the U.S.A 877.407.5847
Toll Free from Mexico 01.800.288.2243
Toll Free from Spain 900.866.949
From other International locations +1.812.671.9757
Fax: 01.812.355.1576
orders@palibrio.com

ISBN:	Softcover	978-1-5065-5161-6
	Ebook	978-1-5065-5162-3

Library of Congress Control Number: 2023922436
Print information available on the last page
Rev date: 29/11/2023

Contents

Dedicated to

1. God, our Creator, and sustainer of all life.
2. The Holy Spirit for insights, guidance, and grace.
3. To all the families, teachers, providers, and friends who love, and support children diagnosed with Autism.
4. To our families who have supported the works that God has led us to fulfill.

Introduction

Sharing information and insights into the real-life story about a mother and her child with a diagnosis of Autism is an extraordinary opportunity for all of us to recognize in order to better understand how loving a child with special needs can be. God loves all, cares for all, and provides all when we ask for His help. We all can put on the lenses of our Creator when seeing others who are different than us. The story of this beautiful child is a tribute to love itself.

The purpose of this book is to provide information to better the quality of life of the people with Autism and their families lives so they can contribute to better our society.

The people who have this condition see how their lives and their families lives are altered by factors such as

1. The lack of a diagnosis
2. The lack of information about the condition of Autism
3. The lack of resources for people with this condition
4. The lack of financial and scientific resources
5. Not knowing the Law and what rights they have as Citizens.
6. The isolation that occurs in different settings

Chapter One

WHAT ARE THE CONDITIONS OF AUTISM SPECTRUM?

Chapter One

What are the Conditions of Autism Spectrum?

There are specific neurological Conditions of Autism Spectrum characterized by a deficit in communication, verbal, social, and motor coordination.

Spectrum means that the conditions affect individuals uniquely and to varying degrees.

The World Health Organization(WHO) is asking all countries to address the problem of early diagnosis since early intervention results in better outcomes. The WHO also addresses the causes of Autism as it links to Human Rights.

What Causes Autism?

The Condition doesn't have a known cause considering the complexity of it and the fact that the symptoms and the severity varies from one individual to another. There are numerous associations. Definitely there is a genetic component that is found in families' genetics. It could be a gene or a generational problem. Is it associated with the measles, mumps, and Rubella (MMR) vaccination? At this time, its hard to say. What do you think?

Diagnosis:

Based on Clinical Observation and History

Early diagnosis changes the outcome of the condition for the individual.

There are questionnaires to help with diagnosing Autism depending on each case.

Treatment for the Behavior and Communication:

In the school setting there are therapeutic interventions that help a child's attention and focus. There are solutions for children that include medicine. It all depends on if it is anxiety related or associated with attention deficit disorder.

Complications:

1. Social isolation
2. Educational isolation
3. Problems with career acquisition and employment

Types of Autism:

1. Classic Autism
2. Mild Autism without mental disorder with a lack of social communication skills
3. Generalized developmental non-specific Autism.
4. Social deficits identified as unable to make friends with peers (the specifications have variations with the publication of the DSM)*
5. Behavior regresses suddenly to infantile level

CLASSIC AUTISM:

(This type is the only one defined here because the other types are self-explanatory.)

These children have difficulties with interests, activities, repetitive behaviors, and limited ability to focus and follow directions. When they are over-stimulated or excited, some children shout words over and over or demonstrate repetitive movements. They are very intelligent and have special creative gifts such as music, art, etc. There is currently no known cure, however, early diagnosis makes a significant difference in multiple areas.

The treatment can include Occupational Therapy, Speech Therapy, and Behavior Therapy.

In the home setting parents can help their child by

1. Building their child's interest
2. Offer a predictable schedule.
3. Teach tasks with a series of simple steps.
4. Actively engage your child's attention in highly structured activities
5. Provide regular reinforcement of good behavior.
6. Parents need to stay involved with every aspect of their child's world.

Can someone with Autism live a normal life?

The answer is yes! They face challenges in daily life but with the right support and resources they can live a fulfilling and meaningful life.

There are big misconceptions about Autism as to not being able to live normal lives. People tend to think that people with Autism are dumb. This is far from the truth.

Chapter Two
FACTS AND STATISTICAL DATA

Chapter Two

Facts and Statistical Data

The number of cases of Autism in the United States seems to be going up because of the services, but more likely because of early diagnosis and better education.

Autism is more frequent in minorities than in Caucasians by 30% according to the CDC. symptoms and the severity vary from one individual to another. There are numerous associations. Definitely, there is a genetic component that is found in families genetics. It could be a gene or a generational problem.

The Condition doesn't have a known cause considering the complexity of it and the fact that the associations. Definitely there is a genetic component that is found in families genetics. It could be a gene or a generational problem.

Is it associated with vaccination (MMR) measles mumps and Rubella? At this time, it's hard to say. What do you think?

Incidence of Prevalence:

Prevalence helps us to understand how many people are currently living with this condition, and it also helps researchers find patterns among different groups of people, (August 22, 2022).

Incidence is the number of people in a population who develop a disease or other health outcome over a period of time (i.e., new cases over a period of time).

The American Psychiatric Association's Diagnostic and Statistical Manual, Fifth Edition (DSM-5) provides Standardized criteria to help diagnose Autism Spectrum.

Types of Screening Tools for the Diagnosis of Autism Spectrum:

1. Ages and Stages Questionnaire (ASQ).
2. Communication and Symbolic Behavior Scale (CSBS).
3. Parents' Evaluation of Developmental Status (PEDS).
4. Modified Checklist of Autism in Toddlers (MCHAT).
5. Screening Tool For Autism in Toddlers and Young Children (STAT).

Chapter Three

MY EXPERIENCE WITH A CHILD WITH AUTISM

Chapter Three

My Experience with a Child with Autism

One day at Church, I first noticed a child running around with a camera taking pictures of everything while he was running around here and there. He would stop and with his fingers would gesture that he was typing something. It was obvious that he wasn't following his mother's directions throughout the service. He followed the Pastor around taking pictures. He removed the Bible from the podium and slammed it on the floor. A woman nearby picked it up and placed it on back where it belonged.

I asked the mother what the child's problem was, and she explained that he was Autistic, refused to eat, and was very active. She continued to detail that he had had a tube in his stomach for feeding since he was 6 months old. According to the mother, his childhood has been the same as her other 2 children. She said the only difference with him was he had no social skills and had not been able to make any friends because he didn't talk.

Due to personal reasons, they didn't have a place to live, so I brought them into my home. That allowed me to observe them as a physician. I realized that he was very curious, that got him into trouble frequently. I also realized that he is intelligent unbeknownst to his mother. According to his mother, sometimes he gets aggressive and has bitten a police officer in the past. He is very loving and has the heart of a much younger child.

We went to the Hispanic festival, and he would play with children by jumping up that got the attention of other children who joined him at first but then left him after they noticed his unusual behavior. He finally sat down and began to eat junk food. The jumping must have aroused or stimulated the stomach and activated his hunger. He finished off two large bags of chips.

He has an atypical fixation on the noise plastic water bottles make and he crushes them. He tears little bits of paper and leaves a trail of them on the floor.

According to the mother he has only attended a couple of months of school in his whole life and he is a 11-years-old. To me, he has an unknow IQ, but I believe it is high. After going through the process of signing him up for a special school that offers curriculum specific to children like him on the Autism Spectrum, his mother took him out of the school because she didn't like something about how a teacher responded to her.

We were able to get him back into the system. Am sure that he is going to do fine there.

Why we should have hope. 1 Peter 1:3, "Blessed be the God and Father of our Lord Jesus Christ, who in his great mercy gave us a new birth to a living hope through the resurrection of Jesus Christ from the dead, to an inheritance that is imperishable...".

This child is active all day long. He has never received treatment or medication. He only sleeps 3-4 hours a night, not long enough to go into a deep brain recovery level sleep. None the less, he is always smiling and seems to be happy.

Further discussion with his mother revealed that her eldest son has Autism but a much milder form. This son was diagnosed at age 10 by his pediatrician confirmed by Autistic testing. His mother claims not wanting to talk about the topic because it is too painful.

Autism and Schizophrenia – Is there a link?

Autism Spectrum and schizophrenia are separate . Both can vary a lot in their symptoms, but both affect how the brain develops.

They may show similar symptoms, but there are key differences that are important to know in order to get a correct diagnosis.

Chapter Four

AMAZING CHILDREN

Chapter Four

Amazing Children

As a therapist for over multiple decades, having worked with individuals on the Autism Spectrum, each child and family have taught me much about the gifts each possess and the challenges they face.

It was the Holy Spirit who helped guide me by revealing what each individual's strengths were as I had the opportunity to spend quality time with each child and on rare occasions, with a group of children on the Spectrum.

These children demonstrate to all of us that they are brave individuals who want to participate in all that life has to offer.

I recall one 8-year-old boy walked in geometric patterns from one point in the clinic to another in the same sequence each time he came for therapy. What could I use to unlock this rigidity and expand his exploration of space?

Another 10-year-old boy was in our T-ball summer program and could hit the ball out of the ballpark, yet he carried the bat all the way to first base. What could I do to help his timing, sequencing, and motor planning?

A group of young teen girls and boys with Asperger's Syndrome participated in our summer theater program where they had to make new friends and help to create a play to perform in front of an audience by the end of the summer. They had quite different personalities, their own behaviors, diverse levels of sensitivity to light, sound, and tolerance to being touched. Each had unique needs and ways of managing this social and more complex environment.

These parents had been looking for ways to provide more age-appropriate life experiences for their children. Once we advertised the program at the clinic, they quickly signed their children up. The purpose of this group was to increase opportunities for teens for peer interaction outside of the school setting. They were all interested in this new social group experience. None of them had ever been involved in putting on a play for an audience to clap for them. This was our first time offering this program in our summer session. How could we tap into each child's strengths while overcoming special needs?

Chapter Five
AMAZING POSSIBILITIES

Chapter Five

Amazing Possibilities

Let me describe to you how the 8-year-old boy who walked in geometric patterns was able to break out of this unusual gait pattern.

I started by working with the child's vestibular system by setting up a bolster swing in the middle of the clinic and when the child mounted the bolster, I sat behind making sure the swing did not tip us off. I broke into a children's song that was coordinated with the timing of the back-and-forth movement of the swing. By the third verse, he was singing the song and later he created his own lyrics in sync with the rhythm of the verse.

The next thing I heard out of this child's mouth was a new melody simply hummed. He smiled contently as he repeated it over and over. I asked him what song he was humming but being a non-verbal communicator, he didn't say anything more.

His mother was in the waiting room, and I called her in to listen and see if she knew what the tune her child was humming. Her child hummed the melody over and over. She said it sounded vaguely familiar... and then it came to her. Her 8-year-old son was singing the melody of the dangling windup music box that was over the bassinet he listened to as an infant while being rocked to sleep. What a trigger swinging and singing was for bringing back an old melody all the way back to his infancy. This auditory memory was his strength, and he was able to express something from a pre-language age. The lullaby had no words and singing together definitely opened up the connection of musical expression in his brain.

That was the very moment the inspiration from the Holy Spirit came to me. I asked his mother if anyone in the family was musical. She replied that neither she nor her husband were musically inclined and there were no instruments in the home. This inspiration continued and I asked if she would consider starting her child in one-one piano classes? She was very excited to think that there was another meaningful activity that she could get her son into. Her hopes, prayers, and wishes for her child were coming to fruition.

The 10-year-old baseball star needed work on timing, sequencing, and motor planning. He needed to practice dropping the bat before running to first base. That was only possible after 5 other teammates took their turns to bat at home plate. I pondered how I was going to help this boy change the pattern of his motor plan and action?

That very day when I got home there was a package in the mail asking me if I was an entrepreneurial type of therapist who was interested in working on timing, sequencing, and motor planning with my clients? There it was...the answer directly from God. I called the company to learn more about this innovative technology and the rest is history. First, I had to train complete the training and then qualify to become a provider of this advanced brain training program myself before I could offer it to clients. This child was one of my first recipients to work on timing, sequencing, and motor planning.

The group of young teens began the first night of the summer theater program by drawing a picture with crayons of their favorite book, character, or movie. The girls each drew their own scenes.

One girl drew a scene from a movie, High School Musical, a Disney 2006 movie directed and choreographed by Kenny Ortega.

Another girl colored a scene from the Disney movie The Little Mermaid that came out in 1989 written and directed by John Musker and Ron Clements. She colored an underwater scene of Little Mermaids.

An older boy drew a scene from his favorite historical character, George Washington, where he was in a ship crossing the Delaware River.

A young boy who loved watching SpongeBob SquarePants that premiered in 1999 on Nickelodeon, was the creation he drew. It was an underwater scene inside the Crabby Patty Café.

A lightbulb went on in my head. Let's create a play using each child's drawing of their favorites to use as the scenery for the different segments of the play. The props were created each week by the kids wearing smocks and painting their larger cardboard canvases .

Chapter Six

AMAZING OUTCOMES

Chapter Six

Amazing Outcomes

The 8-year-old boy started piano lessons and played two pieces on the piano at a church for a talent show where other peers performed. He completely overwhelmed those in the audience that knew him over the years. It made the crowd stand up on their feet and tears rolled down the cheeks of his new fan club.

The 10-year-old baseball star sang a song in front of the audience which filled the room including families, neighbors, providers, and friends in an auditorium. He had a smile on his face and was dressed up in overalls, playing the role of a Railroader working on the Railroad in a talent show as the cardboard train he helped paint rolled on by behind him on stage.

The group of young teens at the end of the summer session performed the play after painting the props they designed and practiced. They each had a role of changing up the props setting the stage for each scene. The weeks of practicing where they were directed to shout their lines so the people in the back rows could hear them flipped on the night of the performance. We didn't see this coming, however the parents did. The actors whispered their lines because that is what they hear coming from the sides of the stage by the play director who was whispering the lines in real time.

There wasn't a dry eye in the audience and each of these performers received their own applause as they entered the stage. This group of teens may have experienced the standing ovation for the first time in their lives as was likely the case for the children in the play at the end of that amazing summer.

I will never forget the feeling and gratitude we all had for the growth these children had this playing and socializing like they did.

Closing Comments

If you haven't picked up one of the powerful messages in this book then perhaps you should read it again more slowly to let the power of what God can do through His inspiration and beautiful music and the amazing brain that He gave us that runs on mental and motor timing, sequencing, and motor planning that opens up to memory, attention and the communication transmission for learning, speaking, and engaging in life skills.

If beautiful music and voices can touch our very soul, then rancid music can damage our Spirit. Listen to the lyrics in popular songs today. They are a death trap for our society and especially for the mentally unstable who might act on what they hear.

The children in this book are real and were touched by incredible music created by outstanding professional instrumentalists that are enthusiastic about expressing themselves through their instrument.

Music needs to come back into our school curriculum along with all of the arts. These are the foundations for training the brain for children with developing brains to express their thoughts and create innovative ideas. When a child watches a video over and over getting stuck and stimming over it, it is blocking their own thoughts and development.

What can you do to enhance and influence your child's growth and development?

We strongly suggest playing easy and calming low-volume Classical instrumental music in the background in your home or while driving in your car. This is essential especially while children are at work doing homework or academic assignments. Be aware of the difference you feel and watch the behavior of your child or children become calm. The loud voices will come down and so will yours. Put the music on softly if fights break out between individuals. Children on the Autism Spectrum are extremely sensitive to their environment.

Call upon the Holy Spirit to fill your home with the Virtues of FAITH, HOPE, CHARITY (LOVE), PEACE, and PATIENCE.

Don't forget KINDNESS and COMPASSION. Teach your children how to pray with you and as a family before meals. Blessing the food these days is especially important.

May God bless all of the readers of this book with His insight for your life and those He gave to you to care for.

If you are inspired and inclined to do so, please visit the website of our non-profit foundation God's Diamonds by searching for

godsdiamonds.net and donate.

May God continue to bless you on your journey to Heaven.

References:

1. Espacio Autismo.com
2. Mexicosocial.org
3. Mayoclinic.com
4. Who.int
5. Mayoclinic.org
6. Espanolnichd.mih.gov
7. Psicologiaymente.com
8. Univeraidodviu.com
9. Bing.com
10. Drsanchezvides.com
11. Autismovivo.org
12. Holy Bible King James version
13. Center Disease Control (CDC) Multiple newsletters

Printed in the United States
by Baker & Taylor Publisher Services